anythink

NO LONGER PROPERTY
OF ANYTHINK
RANGEVIEW LIBRARY
DISTRICT

YOU'RE
THE CHEF

SWEET Cookies AND Bars

Kari Cornell Photographs by Brie Cohen

M MILLBROOK PRESS • MINNEAPOLIS

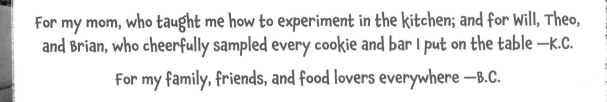

For my mom, who taught me how to experiment in the kitchen; and for Will, Theo, and Brian, who cheerfully sampled every cookie and bar I put on the table —K.C.

For my family, friends, and food lovers everywhere —B.C.

Photography by Brie Cohen
Food in photographs prepared by chef David Vlach
Illustrations by Laura Westlund/Independent Picture Service
The image on page 5 is used with the permission of © iStockphoto.com/stuartbur.

Allergy alert: The recipes in this book contain ingredients to which some people can be allergic. Anyone with food allergies or sensitivities should follow the advice of a physician or other medical professional.

Copyright © 2014 by Lerner Publishing Group, Inc.

All rights reserved. International copyright secured. No part of this book may be reproduced, stored in a retrieval system, or transmitted in any form or by any means—electronic, mechanical, photocopying, recording, or otherwise—without the prior written permission of Lerner Publishing Group, Inc., except for the inclusion of brief quotations in an acknowledged review.

Millbrook Press
A division of Lerner Publishing Group, Inc.
241 First Avenue North
Minneapolis, MN 55401 U.S.A.

Website address: www.lernerbooks.com

Main body text set in Felbridge Std Regular 11/14.
Typeface provided by Monotype Typography.

Library of Congress Cataloging-in-Publication Data

Cornell, Kari A.
Sweet cookies and bars /
by Kari Cornell ; photographs by Brie Cohen.
pages   cm. — (You're the chef)
Includes index.
ISBN 978–0–7613–6638–6 (lib. bdg. : alk. paper)
ISBN 978–1–4677–1714–4 (eBook)
1. Cookies. 2. Desserts. 3. Baking. I. Cohen, Brie, illustrator. II. Title.
TX772.C65928 2014
641.86—dc23   2012048928

Manufactured in the United States of America
1 – CG – 7/15/13

TABLE OF CONTENTS

Before You Start 4

Safety Tips 5

Cooking Tools 6

Techniques 7

Will's Favorite Molasses Cookies—8

All-American Chocolate Chip Cookies—11

Oatmeal Raisin Cookies—14

S'more Graham Cracker Sandwiches—16

Homemade Granola Bars—18

Crispy Rice Cereal Bars—21

Pumpkin Spice Bars—22

Key Lime Bars—25

Halloween Chocolate Brownies—28

Special Ingredients 31

Further Reading and Websites 32

Index 32

Metric Conversions 33

Are you ready to make the sweetest cookies and bars? YOU can be the chef and make delicious treats for yourself and your family. These easy recipes are perfect for a chef who is just learning to cook. And they're so delicious, you'll want to make them again and again!

I developed these recipes with the help of my kids, who are six and eight years old. They can't do all the cooking on their own yet, but they can do a lot.

Can't get enough of cooking? Check out www.lerneresource.com for bonus recipes, healthful eating tips, links to cooking technique videos, and more!

BEFORE YOU START

Reserve your space! Always ask for permission to work in the kitchen.

Find a helper! You will need an adult helper for some tasks. Talk with this person to decide what steps you can do on your own and what steps the adult will help with.

Make a plan! Read through the whole recipe before you start cooking. Do you have the ingredients you'll need? If you don't know what a certain ingredient is, see page 31 to find out more. Do you understand each step? If you don't understand a technique, such as *blend* or *whisk*, turn to page 7. At the beginning of each recipe, you'll see how much time you'll need to prepare the recipe and to cook it. The recipe will also tell you how many servings it makes. Small drawings at the top of each recipe let you know what major kitchen equipment you'll need—such as a stovetop, a mixer, or a microwave.

stovetop

electric mixer

knives

microwave

oven

Wash up! Always wash your hands with soap and water before you start cooking. And wash them again after you touch raw eggs, meat, or fish.

Get it together! Find the tools you'll use, such as measuring cups or a mixing bowl. Gather all the ingredients you'll need. That way you won't have to stop to look for things once you start cooking.

SAFETY TIPS

That's sharp! Your adult helper needs to be in the kitchen when you are using a knife, a grater, or a peeler. If you are doing the cutting, use a cutting board. Cut away from your body, and keep your fingers away from the blade.

That's hot! Be sure an adult is in the kitchen if you use the stove or the oven. Your adult helper can help you cook on the stove and take hot things out of the oven.

Tie it back! If you have long hair, tie it back or wear a hat. If you have long sleeves, roll them up. You want to keep your hair and clothing out of the food and away from flames or other heat sources.

Turn that handle! When cooking on the stove, turn the pot handle toward the back. That way, no one will accidentally bump the pot and knock it off the stove.

Wash it! If you are working with raw eggs or meat, you need to keep things extra clean. After cutting raw meat or fish, wash the knife and the cutting board right away. They must be clean before you use them to cut anything else.

Go slowly! Take your time when you're working. When you are doing something for the first time, such as peeling or grating, be sure not to rush.

Above all, have fun!

Finish the job right!

One of your most important jobs as a chef is to clean up when you're done. Wash the dishes with soap and warm water. Wipe off the countertop or the table. Put away any unused ingredients. The adults in your house will be more excited for you to cook next time if you take charge of cleaning up.

COOKING TOOLS

baking pans

bowls

can opener

cookie sheet

cutting board

dry measuring cups

electric mixer

grater

knives

liquid measuring cup

measuring spoons

oven mitt

rolling pins

rubber scraper

saucepans

spatula

spoon

strainer

table knife

whisk

wire cooling rack

wooden spoon

TECHNIQUES

bake: to cook in the oven

blend: to use an electric mixer or spoon to stir ingredients together until well mixed

boil: to heat liquid on a stovetop until it starts to bubble

chill: to place a food in the refrigerator to make it cold

chop: to cut food into small pieces using a knife

coat: to cover food, a baking pan, or a stovetop pan with a thin layer of oil

grease: to coat a pan in oil or butter so baked food won't stick to the bottom

mix: to stir food using a spoon, a fork, or an electric mixer

preheat: to turn the oven to the temperature you will need for baking. An oven takes about 15 minutes to heat up.

set aside: to put nearby in a bowl or plate or on a clean workspace

slice: to cut food into thin pieces

soften: to remove butter or cream cheese from the refrigerator so it warms up and becomes soft

sprinkle: to scatter on top

whisk: to stir or whip with a whisk or a fork

zest: to remove the very thin, colored layer of skin on citrus fruits

MEASURING

To measure **dry ingredients**, such as sugar or flour, spoon the ingredient into a measuring cup until it is full. Then use the back of a table knife to level it off. Do not pack it down unless the recipe tells you to. Do not use measuring cups made for liquids.

When you're measuring a **liquid**, such as milk or water, use a clear glass or plastic measuring cup. Set the cup on the table or a counter and pour the liquid into the cup. Pour slowly and stop when the liquid has reached the correct line.

Don't measure your ingredients over the bowl they will go into. If you accidentally spill, you might have way too much!

makes 2 dozen cookies

preparation time: 25 minutes
baking time: 7 to 10 minutes
   per sheet of cookies

ingredients:

¼ cup (½ stick) unsalted
   butter, softened
3 cups all-purpose flour
½ teaspoon salt
1 teaspoon baking soda
1 teaspoon ground ginger
½ teaspoon ground cloves
⅛ teaspoon allspice
¼ cup vegetable shortening
½ cup plus ¼ cup sugar
¼ cup light brown sugar
1 egg
¼ cup molasses
2 tablespoons light corn syrup

equipment:

2 medium mixing bowls
measuring cups—1 cup,
   ½ cup, ¼ cup
measuring spoons
electric mixer
whisk
rubber scraper
1 tablespoon
2 cookie sheets
small dish
juice glass
oven mitts
spatula
wire cooling rack

Will's Favorite Molasses Cookies

If you love sweet, rich, spicy cookies, then this is the cookie for you! These stay chewy on the inside and a little crispy on the outside. Mmmm, good!

1. **Remove** the butter from the refrigerator, so it has time to soften.

2. **Place** 2 oven racks near the center of the oven. Then **preheat** the oven to 350°F.

3. In a medium mixing bowl, **combine** flour, salt, baking soda, ground ginger, ground cloves, and allspice. **Mix** well with a whisk, and set aside.

4. In another medium mixing bowl, **add** butter, shortening, ½ cup sugar, and light brown sugar. (Be sure to pack the brown sugar tightly into the measuring cup before adding it to the mixing bowl.) Use an electric mixer to **blend** until creamy.

5. **Crack** the egg into the sugar-butter mixture. **Blend** well with the electric mixer. **Add** light molasses and light corn syrup. **Blend** well.

6. **Add** ⅓ of the flour mixture to the sugar-butter mixture. Use the electric mixer to **blend** well. Repeat 2 more times with the rest of the flour mixture.

Turn the page for more Will's Favorite Molasses Cookies

TRY THIS!

These cookies are delicious dipped in white chocolate. After the cookies have baked and cooled, empty a 12-ounce bag of white chocolate chips into a microwave-safe bowl. Heat the white chocolate on full power for 30 seconds. Then remove and stir. Repeat 2 more times until white chocolate is fully melted. Dip each cookie halfway into the white chocolate. Set cookies on a sheet of parchment or waxed paper to allow to cool and harden.

7. **Measure** ¼ cup sugar into a small, shallow dish. Set it between your bowl of cookie dough and the cookie sheet.

8. Take 1 tablespoon cookie dough in your hands, and **roll** it into a ball. (It should be about the size of a small bouncy ball.) Then **roll** the ball of dough around in the sugar dish until it is completely covered in sugar. **Place** the ball on an ungreased cookie sheet.

9. **Repeat** step 8 for each cookie, until both cookie sheets are filled. The cookies should be placed 2 inches apart on the cookie sheet. Then, with the bottom of a juice glass, **press** down slightly on each ball of dough to flatten it.

10. Use oven mitts to **place** the cookie sheets on the center racks in the oven. **Bake** for 7 to 10 minutes, or until the cookies are puffed and golden. Use oven mitts to **remove** the cookie sheets from the oven. Allow cookies to cool on cookie sheets for 1 minute. Then use a spatula to **place** them on a wire cooling rack to cool completely.

11. **Repeat** steps 8 through 10 until you've used all the dough. Store cooled cookies in an airtight container.

All-American Chocolate Chip Cookies

These cookies are a crisp and buttery version of the popular chocolate chip cookie. Our family uses semisweet chips. But milk chocolate or dark chocolate chips are just as yummy.

1. **Remove** butter from the refrigerator, so it has time to soften.

2. **Place** 2 oven racks near the center of the oven. Then **preheat** the oven to 350°F.

Turn the page for more All-American Chocolate Chip Cookies

makes 2 dozen cookies

preparation time: 20 minutes
baking time: 7 to 9 minutes
per sheet of cookies

ingredients:

1 cup (2 sticks) unsalted butter, softened
2 cups all-purpose flour
½ teaspoon salt
¼ teaspoon cinnamon
½ teaspoon cream of tartar
½ cup sugar
1 cup brown sugar
2 eggs
1½ teaspoons vanilla extract
1 teaspoon baking soda
2 teaspoons hot water
2 cups semisweet chocolate chips

equipment:

2 medium mixing bowls
measuring cups—1 cup, ½ cup
measuring spoons
whisk
electric mixer
small bowl
spoon
wooden spoon
2 cookie sheets
rubber scraper
oven mitts
spatula
wire cooling rack

3. In a medium mixing bowl, combine flour, salt, cinnamon, and cream of tartar. Mix well with a whisk, and set aside.

4. In another medium mixing bowl, **add** softened butter, sugar, and brown sugar. (Be sure to pack the brown sugar tightly into the measuring cup before adding it to the mixing bowl.) Use an electric mixer to **blend** until creamy.

5. **Crack** the eggs into the sugar-butter mixture. **Add** the vanilla extract. **Blend** well with the electric mixer.

6. In a small bowl, **combine** baking soda with hot tap water. Use a spoon to mix well. **Add** the water mixture to the sugar-butter mixture. **Blend** well with an electric mixer.

7. Add ⅓ of the flour mixture to the sugar-butter mixture. **Blend** well with the electric mixer. Repeat 2 more times with the rest of the flour mixture.

8. **Add** semisweet chocolate chips to the dough. **Mix** well with a wooden spoon.

9. **Drop** rounded tablespoons of dough onto an ungreased cookie sheet. Make sure the cookies are 2 inches apart. Repeat with the other cookie sheet.

10. Use oven mitts to **place** the cookie sheets on the center racks in the oven. **Bake** for 7 to 9 minutes, or until golden brown. Use oven mitts to **remove** the cookie sheets from the oven. Allow the cookies to cool for 1 minute on the cookie sheets. Then use a spatula to **place** them on a wire cooling rack to cool completely.

11. **Repeat** steps 9 and 10 until you've used up all the dough. Store the cooled cookies in an airtight container.

TRY THIS!

Combine **semisweet chocolate chips** with **butterscotch** or **peanut butter chocolate chips**, using 1 cup each.

Add ½ cup chopped **walnuts** or **pecans**.

Replace ½ cup flour with ½ cup **rolled oats**.

makes 2 dozen cookies

preparation time: 20 minutes
baking time: 10 minutes per
   sheet of cookies

ingredients:

¾ cup (1½ sticks) unsalted
   butter, softened
⅔ cup all-purpose flour
½ teaspoon salt
1 teaspoon cinnamon
½ teaspoon baking soda
½ cup sugar
1 cup brown sugar
1 egg
2 tablespoons water
1 teaspoon vanilla extract
3 cups quick-cooking oats
1 cup raisins

equipment:

2 medium mixing bowls
measuring cups—1 cup,
   ½ cup, ⅓ cup
measuring spoons
whisk
rubber scraper
electric mixer
wooden spoon
2 cookie sheets
rubber scraper
oven mitts
spatula
wire cooling rack

Oatmeal Raisin Cookies

Oatmeal raisin cookies are a fun way to have the best
of both worlds. They provide a healthy serving of
whole grain oats but still satisfy a sweet tooth.

1. **Remove** the butter from the refrigerator, so it has
   time to soften.

2. **Place** 2 oven racks near the center of the oven.
   Then **preheat** the oven to 350°F.

3. In a medium bowl, **combine** flour, salt,
   cinnamon, and baking soda. **Mix** well
   with a whisk, and set aside.

4. In another medium mixing bowl, **add**
   softened butter, sugar, and brown
   sugar. (Be sure to pack the brown sugar
   tightly into the measuring cup before
   adding to the mixing bowl.) Use an
   electric mixer to **blend** until creamy.

5. **Crack** the egg into the sugar-butter mixture.
   Blend well with the electric mixer. **Add** the
   water and vanilla extract. **Blend** well.

6. **Add** the flour mixture to the sugar-butter mixture, using the
   electric mixer to **blend** well. **Add** oats and raisins to the
   flour mixture. **Stir** with a wooden spoon until well mixed.

7. Use a tablespoon to **scoop** up dough, and **drop** it in rows on a cookie sheet. Make sure cookies are 2 inches apart. Repeat with the other cookie sheet.

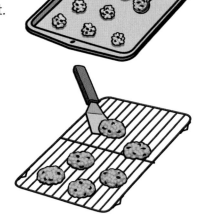

8. Use oven mitts to **place** the cookie sheets on the center racks in the oven. **Bake** for 10 minutes, or until golden brown. Use oven mitts to **remove** the cookie sheets from the oven. Allow the cookies to cool on the cookie sheets for 1 minute. Then use a spatula to **place** them on a wire cooling rack to cool completely.

9. **Repeat** steps 7 and 8 until you've used all the dough. Store cooled cookies in an airtight container.

makes 20 sandwiches

preparation time: 25 minutes
chill time: 2 hours

ingredients:

¼ cup (½ stick) unsalted
  butter, softened
4 ounces cream cheese,
  softened
1 7-ounce jar marshmallow
  creme
20 full-size cinnamon
  graham crackers (about
  2 packages; 3 packages
  come in each box)
2 1.55-ounce chocolate bars

equipment:

medium mixing bowl
electric mixer
rubber scraper
plastic wrap
serving plate
measuring spoons
table knife
airtight container (optional)

S'more Graham Cracker Sandwiches

You won't need a campfire to toast these tasty sandwich cookies—you won't even need a stove or an oven. These no-bake cookies are a cinch to make and taste great.

1. **Remove** the butter and the cream cheese from the refrigerator, so they have time to soften.

2. In a medium mixing bowl, **combine** softened butter and cream cheese. **Mix** well with an electric mixer.

3. Add the entire jar of marshmallow creme. Scrape the jar clean with a rubber scraper. Use an electric mixer to **blend** ingredients well. **Cover** the bowl with plastic wrap. **Place** it in the refrigerator for 2 hours to chill.

4. Prepare the sandwiches. First, carefully **break** a rectangular cracker into two squares along the center dotted line. Then **place** the crackers cinnamon side down on the serving plate. Repeat with the rest of the graham crackers.

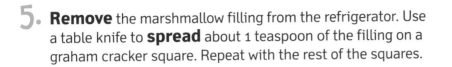

5. **Remove** the marshmallow filling from the refrigerator. Use a table knife to **spread** about 1 teaspoon of the filling on a graham cracker square. Repeat with the rest of the squares.

6. **Break** the chocolate bars into pieces along the break lines. **Place** a piece of chocolate on 20 of the graham cracker squares. Leave the other 20 plain.

7. **Place** 1 plain square facedown on top of a square with chocolate. **Press** down to smoosh the two squares together. Repeat with all the squares to make 20 sandwiches.

8. **Serve** immediately. (These cookies should be eaten as soon as they are made. If you know you won't eat all 20 right away, save the marshmallow filling in an airtight container in the refrigerator to make more later.)

TRY THIS!
If you're not fond of chocolate, use thinly sliced fruit instead. Strawberries or bananas are super tasty.

makes 24 bars

preparation time: 20 minutes
baking time: 10 to 12 minutes
setting time: 2 hours

ingredients:

2 cups old-fashioned rolled oats
½ cup wheat germ
1 cup sliced almonds
½ cup unsalted sunflower
　seeds
¼ cup brown sugar
½ cup honey
3 tablespoons unsalted butter
2 teaspoons vanilla extract
½ teaspoon salt
1 cup shredded coconut
½ cup flaxseeds
1 cup dried cranberries or
　cherries
½ cup white chocolate chips

equipment:

large mixing bowl
measuring cups—1 cup, ½ cup,
　¼ cup
wooden spoon
cookie sheet
oven mitts
9 x 13-inch baking pan
waxed paper
medium saucepan
rubber scraper
cutting board
knife
plastic wrap or airtight
　container

Homemade Granola Bars

These granola bars are a fun, on-the-go snack. And they're packed with healthy whole grains, nuts, and dried fruits. Next time, make your own instead of pulling one from a box!

1. **Preheat** the oven to 350°F.

2. In a large mixing bowl, **combine** rolled oats, wheat germ, sliced almonds, and sunflower seeds. Use a wooden spoon to **mix** well. Use the same spoon to evenly **spread** the oat mixture on a cookie sheet.

3. Use oven mitts to **place** the cookie sheet on the middle rack in the oven. **Bake** for 10 to 12 minutes, or until oats are toasted a golden brown.

4. While the oats are in the oven, **line** a baking pan with sheets of waxed paper. Make sure the waxed paper goes up all four sides of the pan.

5. To a medium saucepan, **add** brown sugar, honey, butter, vanilla extract, and salt. (Be sure to pack the brown sugar tightly into the measuring cup before adding.) Turn the burner under the saucepan on medium. **Stir** the mixture with the wooden spoon, and bring to a boil. **Boil** for 1 minute, stirring constantly. Turn off the burner, and set aside.

6. When the oats are toasted golden brown, turn off the oven. Use oven mitts to **remove** the cookie sheet.

*Turn the page for more
Homemade Granola Bars*

TRY THIS!

Add your own favorite **dried fruits** or **nuts**. Peanuts and raisins are a classic combination. Also try chopped **dried apricots, dates, or dried blueberries.**

Add ½ teaspoon **cinnamon** to the rolled oats after they've been toasted.

Homemade Granola Bars continued

7. Have an adult pour the toasted oats into the large mixing bowl. **Pour** the heated honey-sugar mixture over the oats. Then **add** coconut, flaxseeds, and dried cranberries or cherries. **Stir** carefully with the wooden spoon. Make sure all the dry pieces are completely coated with the honey-sugar mixture.

8. **Add** the white chocolate chips to the oats mixture. **Stir** to combine.

9. Use a rubber scraper to **put** the sticky oat mixture into the baking pan. **Spread** the mixture evenly as best you can with the scraper or the wooden spoon.

10. Tear off 1 large sheet of waxed paper. **Place** it on top of the oats in the pan so that the entire mixture is covered. Place an oven mitt on top of the waxed paper. Then use your hands to **press** hard on the oat mixture. Move the oven mitt around so you can **push** the mixture into all four corners of the pan.

11. Allow the mixture to **cool** for 2 hours. When cool, carefully pull off the top layer of waxed paper. **Pull** up on the edges of the bottom layer of waxed paper to **remove** the bars. **Flip** the bars over onto a cutting board. The waxed paper side will be on top. Carefully peel the paper off. Use a knife to **cut** the mixture into bars. Store in an airtight container, or wrap each bar in plastic wrap.

Crispy Rice Cereal Bars

This old-fashioned treat gets a new twist when you add mini M&M candies or peanut butter chips. Enjoy!

makes 16 bars

preparation time:
15 minutes
cooking time:
3 to 5 minutes

ingredients:
cooking spray
2 ¾ cups mini
marshmallows (half
of a 10-ounce bag)
3 tablespoons
unsalted butter
1 teaspoon vanilla
1 tablespoon
flaxseeds
3 cups crispy rice
cereal, such as Rice
Krispies
¾ cup mini M&Ms,
mini chocolate
chips, or peanut
butter chips

equipment:
8-inch square
baking pan
medium saucepan
wooden spoon
measuring spoons
measuring cups—
1 cup, ¼ cup
rubber scraper
knife

1. **Coat** a baking pan with a thin layer of cooking spray. Set aside.

2. In a medium saucepan, **add** mini marshmallows and butter. Turn the burner under the saucepan on medium. **Melt** the marshmallows and butter, stirring every once in a while with a wooden spoon.

3. When marshmallows and butter are completely melted, turn off the burner. **Add** vanilla, and **stir** to mix well. **Add** flaxseeds, cereal, and M&Ms or chips. **Stir** well with the wooden spoon.

4. Use a rubber scraper to **put** the cereal mix in the baking pan. **Press** the mixture into all corners of the pan. Allow the bars to cool completely. **Cut** them into squares and serve.

makes 24 bars

preparation time: 15 minutes
baking time: 20 to 25 minutes

ingredients:

3 ounces cream cheese, softened
1 cup (2 sticks) plus 2 tablespoons
   unsalted butter, softened
3 eggs
1 cup canned pumpkin puree
2 cups plus 1 tablespoon
   all-purpose flour
1½ cups brown sugar
½ teaspoon salt
1½ teaspoons cinnamon
½ teaspoon ground ginger
¼ teaspoon ground cloves
1 teaspoon baking soda
1 teaspoon baking powder
1 cup raisins
cooking spray
¾ cup powdered sugar
1 teaspoon vanilla extract

equipment:

microwave-safe bowl
large mixing bowl
electric mixer
can opener
rubber scraper
medium mixing bowl
measuring cups—1 cup,
   ½ cup, ¼ cup
measuring spoons
wooden spoon
9 x 13-inch baking pan
oven mitts
toothpick
knife

Pumpkin Spice Bars

Here's a perfect treat for a crisp, fall afternoon.
For a festive touch, sprinkle Halloween cookie
decorations over the frosting.

1. **Remove** the cream cheese from the
   refrigerator, so it has time to soften. Also
   remove 2 tablespoons butter to soften.

2. **Place** 1 oven rack in the center position in
   the oven. Then **preheat** the oven to 350°F.

3. **Put** 1 cup butter in a microwave-safe bowl. Place the
   bowl in the microwave, and **heat** for 30 seconds, or
   until butter is melted. Use oven mitts to **remove** the
   bowl from the microwave. Allow to cool slightly.

4. **Crack** eggs into a large mixing bowl.
   Use an electric mixer to **whisk** the
   eggs on low for 1 minute.

5. **Add** melted butter and canned
   pumpkin puree to the eggs. Use
   the electric mixer to **mix** for 1
   minute, or until well combined.

6. In a medium mixing bowl, **add** 2 cups flour, brown sugar, salt, cinnamon, ground ginger, ground cloves, baking soda, and baking powder. (Be sure to pack the brown sugar tightly into the measuring cup before adding.) **Stir** with a wooden spoon to mix.

7. **Add** the flour mixture to the pumpkin mixture. **Mix** well with the electric mixer. **Add** raisins. **Stir** with the wooden spoon.

8. **Coat** the bottom and sides of a baking pan with a thin layer of cooking spray. Then **sprinkle** the pan with 1 tablespoon flour. Carefully **shake** and **turn** the pan, so the flour covers the bottom, corners, and sides of the pan.

9. Use the rubber scraper to **put** the pumpkin batter into the baking pan. **Spread** the batter evenly onto the bottom of the pan. Use the rubber scraper or wooden spoon to push it to all four corners.

Turn the page for more Pumpkin Spice Bars

TRY THIS!
Add ½ cup chopped **pecans** or **walnuts** when you add the raisins. Or leave out the raisins altogether.

10. Use oven mitts to **place** the pan in the oven. **Bake** for 20 to 25 minutes, or until done. (To check if the bars are done, remove the pan from the oven with oven mitts. Stick a toothpick in the center of the pan. If the toothpick comes out clean, the bars are done. If crumbs cling to the toothpick, cook the bars for another 5 minutes.)

11. While the bars bake, **wash** and dry the medium mixing bowl, the electric mixer beaters, and the rubber scraper.

12. **Place** the softened cream cheese, 2 tablespoons butter, powdered sugar, and vanilla extract in the mixing bowl. Mix well with the electric mixer.

13. Use oven mitts to **remove** the pumpkin bars from the oven. Use the rubber scraper to spread frosting on the warm bars. Allow the bars to cool completely. **Cut** into squares and serve.

Key Lime Bars

These sour and sweet bars are a tasty treat in the spring or summer. Regular limes are just fine. But if you can find key limes, use them!

1. **Remove** the butter from the refrigerator, so it has time to soften.

2. **Place** 1 oven rack in the center position in the oven. Then **preheat** the oven to 350°F.

3. To prepare the crust, **combine** cinnamon, flour, and graham cracker crumbs in a medium mixing bowl. **Stir** with a whisk to blend together well.

Turn the page for more Key Lime Bars

makes 16 bars

preparation time: 15 minutes
total baking time: 40 minutes

ingredients:
Crust:
¼ cup (½ stick) unsalted butter, softened
¼ teaspoon cinnamon
¼ cup all-purpose flour
¾ cup graham cracker crumbs
¼ cup sugar
cooking spray

Topping:
1 regular lime or 2 key limes
3 large eggs
¾ cup sugar
3 tablespoons all-purpose flour
½ teaspoon baking powder
⅛ teaspoon salt
2 teaspoons powdered sugar

equipment:
medium mixing bowl
measuring spoons
measuring cup—¼ cup
whisk
2 medium mixing bowls
electric mixer
rubber scraper
8-inch square baking pan
oven mitts
wire cooling rack (optional)
grater
cutting board
knife
small bowl
spoon
liquid measuring cup
small mesh strainer

Key Lime Bars continued

4. In a medium mixing bowl, **add** butter and sugar. Use an electric mixer to **blend** the butter and the sugar together, until light and fluffy.

5. **Add** half the flour mixture to the butter and sugar mixture. Use the electric mixer to **blend** well. Turn off the mixer, and add the second half of the flour. Use the electric mixer to blend.

6. **Coat** the bottom and sides of a baking pan with cooking spray. Use the rubber scraper to **put** the dough into the pan. **Spread** the dough evenly into all four corners of the pan.

7. Use oven mitts to **place** the pan on the center rack in the oven. **Bake** for 15 minutes. When the crust is done, **remove** the baking pan from the oven. Set on a wire cooling rack to cool.

8. While the crust cools, begin the topping. Wash the lime. Use the small holes of a grater to **zest** the lime. (If you are using key limes, use 2 limes here.) Be careful not to grind off too much of the white pith just under the green layer of skin. It tastes bitter. Set aside.

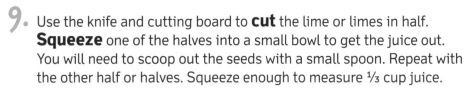

9. Use the knife and cutting board to **cut** the lime or limes in half. **Squeeze** one of the halves into a small bowl to get the juice out. You will need to scoop out the seeds with a small spoon. Repeat with the other half or halves. Squeeze enough to measure ⅓ cup juice.

10. **Crack** the eggs into a medium mixing bowl. Use the electric mixer to **whisk** until foamy. **Add** ¾ cup sugar, lime zest, lime juice, 3 tablespoons flour, baking powder, and salt. Whisk with the electric mixer until well combined.

11. Pour the filling into the baked crust. Use oven mitts to **place** the pan back in the oven. **Bake** for 25 minutes, or until the filling doesn't jiggle when you move the pan.

12. Use oven mitts to **remove** the pan from the oven. Place the pan on the wire cooling rack. Cool completely. Measure the powdered sugar into a small mesh strainer. Gently **shake** the sugar in the strainer evenly over the top of the bars. **Slice** into squares and enjoy!

TRY THIS!

Substitute other citrus fruits for the lime. **Lemon** bars are favorites, but **orange** bars are yummy too. Just make sure you zest about 1 tablespoon of outer skin and squeeze ⅓ cup juice.

If you can't find premade graham cracker crumbs, make your own. Place a few whole graham crackers in a ziplock bag, and crush them with the back of a spoon on a cutting board.

An all-flour crust can be used instead of the graham cracker crust. Just replace the amount of graham cracker crumbs with the same amount of flour.

makes 16 bars

preparation time: 20 minutes
baking time: 25 minutes

ingredients:

cooking spray
5 tablespoons unsalted butter
1 ounce bittersweet or
    semisweet baking chocolate
⅔ cup unsweetened cocoa
1¼ cups sugar
1 cup all-purpose flour
½ teaspoon baking powder
½ teaspoon salt
3 eggs
1 teaspoon vanilla extract
4 mini candy bars, any kind

equipment:

large saucepan
wooden spoon
measuring cups—1 cup,
    ⅓ cup, ¼ cup
2 medium mixing bowls
measuring spoons
whisk
rubber scraper
8-inch square baking pan
oven mitts
toothpick
knife
cutting board

Halloween Chocolate Brownies

Do you like fudgy, rich brownies that melt in your mouth? Then you'll love this recipe. Adding candy bar pieces at the end is a great way to use up some of your Halloween candy!

1. **Place** 1 oven rack in the center position in the oven. Then **preheat** the oven to 350°F. **Coat** a baking pan with a thin layer of cooking spray.

2. In a large saucepan, **add** unsalted butter and baking chocolate. Turn the burner under the saucepan on medium. Use a wooden spoon to **stir** the butter and the chocolate until melted.

3. **Add** unsweetened cocoa to the saucepan, and **stir** to combine. Cook for 1 minute. **Add** sugar to the saucepan, and **stir** to combine. Cook for 1 minute. Turn off the burner, and set the saucepan aside.

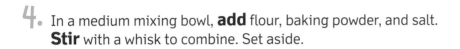

4. In a medium mixing bowl, **add** flour, baking powder, and salt. **Stir** with a whisk to combine. Set aside.

5. In a second mixing bowl, **crack** the eggs. **Whisk** the eggs with a whisk until well combined.

Turn the page for more Halloween Chocolate Brownies

TRY THIS!

If you don't have any mini candy bars on hand, leave them out. The brownies taste just as great without them.

Add ½ cup chopped walnuts in step 7.

6. Use a rubber scraper to **add** ⅓ of the chocolate mixture to the eggs. **Stir** with a wooden spoon to mix well. **Repeat** 2 more times with the rest of the chocolate mixture. **Add** the vanilla extract, and **stir** well.

7. **Add** the flour mixture to the chocolate-egg mixture. **Stir** with the wooden spoon until well blended. Do not overmix. Use the rubber scraper to **put** the brownie mixture into the pan.

8. Use a knife and a cutting board to **chop** four mini chocolate bars into tiny pieces. **Sprinkle** these pieces evenly across the top of the brownie batter.

9. Use oven mitts to **place** the pan in the center of the oven. **Bake** for 25 minutes, or until done. To check if the brownies are done, remove the pan from the oven with the oven mitts. Stick a toothpick in the center of the pan. If the toothpick comes out nearly clean, the brownies are done. If unbaked batter clings to the toothpick, cook the brownies for another 5 minutes. Do not overbake, though. Otherwise, the brownies will be dry and crumbly.

10. Allow the brownies to cool completely. **Cut** them into squares and serve.

SPECIAL INGREDIENTS

bittersweet or semisweet baking chocolate: a type of chocolate that is sweet, but not too sweet. Look for bars of bittersweet or semisweet baking chocolate in the baking aisle of most grocery stores.

cooking spray: a vegetable oil spray that keeps food from sticking to cookie sheets and pans. Cooking spray can be found in the baking aisle of most grocery stores.

corn syrup: a sweet, clear syrup made from corn. Corn syrup is located in the baking aisle of most grocery stores.

flaxseeds: small brown or golden seeds from the flax plant. Look for flaxseeds in the bulk section or health food section of your grocery store or food co-op.

graham cracker crumbs: crumbs made from graham crackers. They are sold in boxes in the baking aisle of most grocery stores.

key limes: tiny limes that grow in the Florida Keys. These limes are a bit more sour than the bigger, more common Persian limes. They also have a smoother skin. Key limes can be found in the produce section of most grocery stores.

marshmallow creme: a sweet, creamy spread made with egg whites, sugar, and vanilla flavoring. Jars of marshmallow creme can be found in the baking aisle of the grocery store.

molasses: a thick, brown syrup that is made from sugar. Look for molasses with other syrups in the grocery store.

shredded coconut: the shredded white insides of a coconut. Shredded coconut is sold in bags in the baking aisle of most grocery stores.

unsweetened cocoa: a powder made from ground cocoa beans. Cocoa beans are also used to make chocolate. Unsweetened cocoa can be found in the baking aisle of most grocery stores.

vanilla extract: liquid vanilla flavor. You can find vanilla in the baking section of the grocery store. Most stores sell both pure vanilla extract and artificially flavored extract. Either type will work.

vegetable shortening: a solid fat made from vegetable oils that is commonly used in pastries and other baked items. Look for shortening in the baking aisle of the store.

wheat germ: a portion of the wheat kernel that is filled with nutrients. Look for wheat germ in a jar in the baking aisle of the grocery store.

FURTHER READING AND WEBSITES

Abrams, Michelle, and Glenn Abrams. *The Kids-Did-It! Cookie Bookie: A (Fun) Cookie-Baking Cookbook for Kids, Illustrated by Kids!* San Diego: CreateSpace, 2009. This cookie cookbook is filled with creative recipes for kids.

Choose My Plate
http://www.choosemyplate.gov/children-over-five.html
Play a game about making healthy food choices or print out coloring pages about nutrition at this website.

Cleary, Brian P. *Food Is CATegorical series.* Minneapolis: Millbrook Press, 2011. This seven-book illustrated series offers a fun introduction to the food groups and other important health information.

Nissenberg, Sandra. *The Everything Kids' Cookbook: From Mac 'n Cheese to Double Chocolate Chip Cookies—90 Recipes to Have Some Finger-Lickin' Fun.* Avon, MA:

LERNER SOURCE™
Expand learning beyond the printed book. Download free, complementary educational resources for this book from our website, www.lerneresource.com.

Adams Media, 2008. This cookbook is a great source for recipes kids love to make, including many cookie recipes.

Recipes
http://www.sproutonline.com/crafts-and-recipes/recipes
Find more fun and easy recipes for kids at this site.

Saulsbury, Camilla V. *No-Bake Cookies: More Than 150 Fun, Easy & Delicious Recipes for Cookies, Bars, and Other Cool Treats Made Without Baking.* Nashville: Cumberland House Publishing, 2006. This cookbook is filled with no-bake recipes for sweet treats.

INDEX

almonds, 18

bar recipes, 18, 21, 22, 25, 28
brownies, 28
butterscotch chips, 13

candy, 21, 28
cherries, dried, 18
chocolate, 21; bars, 16; semisweet, 11, 28; white, 9, 18
cinnamon, 11, 14, 22, 25
cloves, 8, 22
coconut, 18
cookie recipes, 8, 11, 14, 16
cooking preparation, 4
cooking techniques, 7

cooking tools, 6
cranberries, dried, 18
cream cheese, 16, 22

frosting, 22
fruits, dried, 18

ginger, 8, 22
graham crackers, 16, 25
granola, 18

limes, 25

marshmallow, 16, 21
measuring, 7
molasses, 8

no-bake recipes, 16, 21

oats, 13, 14, 18

peanut butter chips, 13, 21
pecans, 13, 23
pumpkin, 22

raisins, 14, 22

safety, 5
s'mores, 16
special ingredients, 31

vanilla extract, 11, 14, 18, 21, 22, 28

walnuts, 13, 23, 30

You're the Chef
Metric Conversions

VOLUME

⅛ teaspoon	0.62 milliliters
¼ teaspoon	1.2 milliliters
½ teaspoon	2.5 milliliters
¾ teaspoon	3.7 milliliters
1 teaspoon	5 milliliters
½ tablespoon	7.4 milliliters
1 tablespoon	15 milliliters
⅛ cup	30 milliliters
¼ cup	59 milliliters
⅓ cup	79 milliliters
½ cup	118 milliliters
⅔ cup	158 milliliters
¾ cup	177 milliliters
1 cup	237 milliliters
2 quarts (8 cups)	1,893 milliliters
3 fluid ounces	89 milliliters
12 fluid ounces	355 milliliters
24 fluid ounces	710 milliliters

MASS (weight)

1 ounce	28 grams
3.4 ounces	96 grams
3.5 ounces	99 grams
4 ounces	113 grams
7 ounces	198 grams
8 ounces	227 grams
12 ounces	340 grams
14.5 ounces	411 grams
15 ounces	425 grams
15.25 ounces	432 grams
16 ounces (1 pound)	454 grams
17 ounces	482 grams
21 ounces	595 grams

TEMPERATURE

Fahrenheit	Celsius
170°	77°
185°	85°
250°	121°
325°	163°
350°	177°
375°	191°
400°	204°
425°	218°
450°	232°

LENGTH

¼ inch	0.6 centimeters
½ inch	1.27 centimeters
1 inch	2.5 centimeters
2 inches	5 centimeters
3 inches	7.6 centimeters
5 inches	13 centimeters
8 inches	20 centimeters
9 x 11 inches	23 x 28 centimeters
9 x 13 inches	23 x 33 centimeters